★ REAL
★ WOMEN
★ NEVER
★ PUMP
★ IRON

REAL WOMEN NEVER PUMP IRON

By
Lisa Chambers
Illustrated by
Alyse Newman

TRiBECA
COMMUNICATIONS, INC.
New York

Acknowledgements

Without the inspiring example of such Real Women as Joan of Arc, Elizabeth Taylor, Julia Child, Eleanor Roosevelt, and Mary Tyler Moore, this book could never have been written. A thousand thanks also go to my editor, Gail MacColl, for her patience, sympathy, and intelligence; to Alyse Newman for capturing the fun of being a Real Woman in her cartoons; and to Vanessa Trueblood, Nan Lawless, Pamela Wheelwright, and hundreds of others for sharing their insights into the real nature of Real Womanhood with me, and for giving generously of their time and expertise. Finally, thanks are due to Phil for being right—at least about this book— and to Ken for helping with the typing.

ISBN-0-943392-10-1

Produced by Philip Lief & Associates
Southfield, MA 01259 USA

Printed in the United States of America

Table of Contents

★ ★ ★ ★ ★ ★ ★ ★ ★ ★ ★ ★ ★ ★ ★ ★ ★ ★

★ ★ ★ ★ ★ ★ ★ ★ ★ ★ ★ ★ ★ ★ ★ ★ ★

Introduction

★ ★ ★ ★ ★ ★ ★ ★ ★ ★ ★ ★ ★ ★ ★ ★ ★

Not long ago, I landed an assignment to do a story on Real Women and Other Endangered Species. At first I thought it would be a snap; I would simply interview several of my women friends and write the article. But as I began to think more about the subject, and to discuss it with people, my doubts grew. Who was a Real Woman and who wasn't? Everyone I knew seemed to have a different idea, and I became increasingly confused. In desperation I returned to the editor who had given me the assignment.

"Frankly, I'm at a loss as to where to begin," I admitted.

"I know, Lisa," she said sympathetically. "It's not an easy subject to write about these days . . . . But I have an idea. Talk to Vanessa Trueblood. She's the president of Consolidated Products, Inc., and yet she still manages to be so—so utterly feminine. Try to find out how she does it."

How indeed, I wondered as I dropped off my last fare, switched on the "off duty" sign, and headed the cab toward the Corporate Women's Health Club in midtown Manhattan. How, in these confusing times, did a woman manage to take Wall Street by storm, serve Cordon Bleu dinners for twelve, know the difference between a de la Renta and a Bill Blass in three seconds or less, have multiple orgasms, write her Congressman, and still murmur sweet nothings into her lover's ear?

Vanessa Trueblood was on the balance beam when I entered the posh gym. As I watched, spellbound, she executed a beautiful back handstand into a split. I made a note of that, and then tried to think of a good opening question. Glancing around the gym, my eyes fell on a set of barbells. "Do Real Women—ah—pump iron?" I asked. Vanessa gave me a blank look. As I soon discovered, iron meant one of three things to her: (1) an essential part of every woman's diet that she needs more of than men; (2) something that should be done to clothes before they are worn even if the label says Permanent Press; (3) the kind of lady Margaret Thatcher is.

To help her understand what *I* meant by iron, I seized a barbell and lifted it to the level of her large, hazel eyes. Vanessa shook her head reprovingly. "Real Women don't pump that kind of iron, because if you do you sweat. There is no other word for it. If you lift heavy barbells for a very long time, your body will be swathed in sweat, which will roll in rivulets down your face and figure. This breaks a sacrosanct rule which goes like this: Horses sweat, men perspire, women feel the heat, Real Women glow."

I looked at her. She was glowing, all right. In fact, with her trim, athletic figure, confident manner, winning smile, and marvelous cheekbones, she reminded me of Katharine Hepburn after she had just teed off in *Pat and Mike*.

"Well, I have to be going now," she said as I continued to stand there, gaping. "Robert DeNiro's coming to dinner and I'm making quiche."

"But I thought—" I stammered, letting the barbell drop with a thud to the floor. What was this woman telling me? After all, there was *that* book.

Vanessa flashed me her most radiant smile. "Let me tell you a secret, Lisa," she said. "Real Women cook quiche from scratch and make real men eat it."

I was so stunned by this revelation that I forgot to put on the meter for my next fare. But it didn't matter: In a week I changed my job, my address, and my hairstyle. And wrote this book, which is dedicated to Vanessa and Real Women everywhere.

Real Woman Q & A

★ ★ ★ ★ ★ ★ ★ ★ ★ ★ ★ ★ ★ ★ ★ ★ ★

Q. How many Real Women does it take to change a light bulb?

A. None. Real Women dine by candlelight.

"*The more G. Q. he gets, the more Frederick's I get.*"

★ THE
★ REAL
★ WOMAN
★ LOOK

Fashion and The Real Woman

The Real Woman tries to avoid looking like Diane Von Furstenberg. Which is to say she tries to avoid looking like a man-eating fish, a barracuda, let's say. She also tries to avoid looking like a man. This is no easy task when the current trend in clothes design is to disguise all hint of secondary sexual characteristics. The Real Woman suspects a lot of clothes designers are embarrassed about the anatomical differences between men and women. She is not.

Nor is the Real Woman on a perpetual tryout for Ringling Bros.—she generally steers clear of Perry Ellis and Norma Kamali. She tends to think Halston is great for Liza but she would much rather have five jean skirts from Calvin Klein.

The Real Woman does not dress in "attitudes." She leaves that to Valley Girls, rock stars' lady friends, *New York Times* book reviewers and other people with time on their hands.

Real Women do not wear satin jumpsuits, fur pants or ultrasuede anything.

Real Women do not subscribe to the bruised look. They do not sport red eyelids, blue hair or yellow lips. They do not apply blush in vivid little circles so as to look like victims of tuberculosis.

Real Women do not wear fake furs.

Real Women do not wear wigs unless they are in costume for the stage or Halloween.

Real Women wear 100% cotton underwear. Only the naive or foolhardy woman ventures into the world of polyester/Lycra panties.

Real Women do own funny undergarments—sexy little things given to them by boyfriends or by girlfriends at engagement showers. A black satin ensemble for special occasions is fine.

Real Women do not wear babushkas, coolie hats, or gimme caps unless they are Russian, Oriental or drive a truck for a living.

Real Women have profited from Gloria Steinem's example. They have seen the folly of sporting high-profile eyewear. They stick to the straight and narrow when shopping for glasses.

Real Women wear bras. But never a black bra under a white blouse, and never a bra designed by the Army Corps of Engineers—that kind of support they don't need.

Real Women who wear men's clothing make sure it's the real thing. Button-down shirts from Brooks Brothers, shetland sweaters from Paul Stuart, cotton T-shirts from Fruit-of-the-Loom.

Real Women who don't live in California do not go food-shopping in tennis whites, golf outfits, or jogging warm-ups.

Real Women do not look like jewelry counters or ore mines. This means no huge, globular sculptures hanging off ears or chests or wrists. Real Women also eschew the cowbell syndrome—they do not wear excessively noisy jewelry like ten spangle bracelets so that their every movement is amplified for the benefit of the entire universe.

Real Women do not wear white to other women's weddings. Or black.

Real Women do not wear T-shirts with small print lettering. They do not like to see men squinting at their breasts. ✦

Real Women do not wear aviator jackets, glasses, scarves or helmets unless they are (1) licensed pilots or (2) direct descendants of Lafayette Escadrille flyers.

Real Women think pin-stripe suits are fine. On men. If they work in an office they wear dresses from Albert Nipon or skirts from L. L. Bean. They own one navy wool suit for interviews.

Real Women try to avoid fashion extremes. Black boots, for instance, are great. Black boots with leather pants with a studded belt and black silk shirt is not great. In fact, S&M emblems like studded jeans and belts definitely edge into iron-pumping territory. By the same token, Real Women consider the opposite effect—the girlish femininity of a Laura Ashley dress with ribbons in the hair and Mary Janes on the feet—false advertising.

Real Women do not allow fashion to take them across the threshold of pain. They do not wear shoes with four-inch heels, they do not wear skin-tight jeans.

Basically, the Real Woman is confident enough not to drown herself in someone else's look. She doesn't parade designer labels, but she's not embarrassed by them either. She likes to have fun, but she doesn't like to look silly. Attractive is fine, frilly or frumpy are extreme. The Real Woman likes to leave some details of her figure to the imagination and the privacy of the bedroom. She doesn't strut her stuff in public. She doesn't need to.

What The Real Woman Never Wears

1. A girdle.

2. A polyester pants suit.

3. Falsies.

Real Woman Talk

Sounding like a Real Woman is every bit as important as dressing like one. The operative word here is "woman"—Real Women do not talk like thirteen-year-old girls.

They do not use phrases like *to the max* or *gag me with a spoon.* Disgusting things are not *grody* or *yucky;* wonderful things are not *tubular* or *awesome.* They do not ditch men by saying *bag your face*—they say "excuse me, I have to leave." The socially unacceptable person is just that, not a *beastie.* Boring is boring, not *beige.* Utterly missing from the Real Woman's vocabulary is the rejoinder *fer sure.* The Real Woman says "certainly," "definitely" or "of course." Moreover:

The Real Woman does not describe her fellow female workers as *great gals.*

The Real Woman does not *go for it.* Neither does anyone she knows. The Real Woman is impressed, not *blown away.*

The Real Woman gets drunk or smashed, occasionally bombed. She never gets *twisted, blasted, polluted,* or *shit-faced.* She gets high, not *wasted.*

The Real Woman does not speak in diminutives or cute euphemisms. *Thingie, tushie, marvy, delish*—this sort of talk will not do. She uses the bathroom or the john, never the *little girls' room.* She goes to sleep, not *beddy-bye.* She does not use abbreviations like A. T. D., C. B. C., or T. N. T.

The Real Woman makes love or has sex. She does not *hide salamis*, go for *rolls in the hay, play Mommy and Daddy*, or *get some*. She kisses. She likes to kiss. She does not like to *chew* or *suck face, smash mouth* or *swap spit*. By the way, the Real Woman finds that relationships come in three sizes: on again/off again, intense, and married.

The Real Woman does not *make tracks, get psyched, harbor doubts*, or *lose her cool*. She is not *into* anything, she does not do things *in a big way*.

The Real Woman takes it easy. She relaxes. She does not *hang out, mellow out, get loose* or *get mellow*. Sometimes the Real Woman daydreams. But she doesn't *space, zone*, or *get fogged in*.

The Real Woman is never *on the rag*. She usually is getting, has, or has just gotten over her period.

The Real Woman's staple word of praise is "cute." Men are cute, items of clothing are cute, ideas are cute. Entire European countries are cute.

The sound of the Real Woman is almost as important as her choice of words. The Real Woman does not drawl, slur, whine or mince her words. Just as baby talk is for babies so sugary sweet talk is for sugar daddies. And Real Women don't need sugar daddies.

Finally, the Real Woman does not swear like a man. Despite seeming permissiveness in this area, she only feels comfortable using "shit." The Real Woman is willing to "give someone some shit," for instance. She is capable of conceding that "the shit" occasionally "hits the fan." Further than this she will not go.*✶

---

*This does not mean the Real Woman doesn't know the bad word vocabulary—in selected circumstances she can "talk dirty" to beat the band.

.

What The Real Woman Will Never Do at a Formal Affair

★ ★ ★ ★ ★ ★ ★ ★ ★ ★ ★ ★ ★ ★ ★ ★ ★

1. **Dance alone.** (Or with other women after the first fifteen minutes.)

2. **Get into a chug-a-lug contest.**

3. **Roll joints.**

4. **Leave just when the fun starts because she has to get up early.***

* The Real Woman is also never, *ever*, the last person to leave a party.

Real Woman Q & A

★ ★ ★ ★ ★ ★ ★ ★ ★ ★ ★ ★ ★ ★ ★ ★

Q. How does a Real Woman tell the difference between an Extra-Terrestrial and Richard Gere?

A. If they look that much alike, why bother?

"*As a Real Woman I can fart in the elevator and everyone thinks it is someone else.*"

★ REAL
★ WOMAN'S
★ NITTY
★ GRITTY

Real Women vs. Iron Pumpers

A Real Woman has to be ambitious, accomplished, enduring, attractive—and underneath it all have a heart of gold and a good credit rating. Not everyone can make the grade.

There are so many pretenders to the throne, so many false witnesses, so many unlicensed practitioners—how can we possibly know the genuine from the ersatz?

How can the ordinary woman—or man— on the street tell the fakers from the real thing? Amongst all the subtle and extensive variations on femaleness and femininity, how can you, a lone assessor, without compass or full-time professional guidance, avoid being fooled, tricked, or otherwise taken in by the heady imitators of greatness?

Be of good faith. A single determining factor has been isolated and brought to light. It seems the world of women may be divided with a single stroke between those who pump iron, and those who don't. With only this one guideline in mind the qualifications of any candidate for Real Woman status can be speedily, and summarily, assessed.

Jeane Kirkpatrick, for instance, pumps iron.

Golda Meir never did.

Blonde of all blondes Marilyn Monroe wouldn't even look at a barbell; scrawny successors like Morgan Fairchild and Farrah Fawcett-Majors have hair that dead lifts 200.

Glenda Jackson—oh, that condescending sneer—is a Real Woman. So are Bette Midler, Colleen Dewhurst, Jodie Foster (extra points for grace under pressure), Chris Evert Lloyd.

Christie Hefner is a Real Woman for taking over her Dad's business and running it better than he did. Katherine Graham is a Real Woman for taking over her husband's business and running it better than he did. Martina Navratilova, Nancy Lieberman, Bette Stove and Rosie Casals are hopelessly devoted iron-pumpers. The jury is still out on Hana Mandlikova.

Loretta Lynn—the Queen of Country Music—does not pump iron.

Mary Tyler Moore does not pump iron.

Dolly Parton does not pump iron.

Arlene Dahl can do it with one plump little finger. So can Dinah Shore—is this why she and Burt didn't work out? Barbara Walters does it between interviews.

Rosalynn Carter may have pumped iron; Nancy Reagan certainly does. Eleanor Roosevelt never touched the stuff.

Rita Jenrette is rumored to have done it on the steps of the Capitol Building.

Dr. Ruth Westheimer can pump iron with her vocal chords.

Mary Cunningham started doing it after William Agee accepted her resignation from Bendix Corp.; she stopped after William Agee married her.

Rene Richards and Jan Morris are de facto iron pumpers, as was Christine Jorgensen before them.

Barbra Streisand will heft a few if it means she gets to direct her own movies. Jane Fonda has just taken it up.

Ann Miller can pump iron but only with her make-up on. Diane Keaton would except that it's so tacky. Meryl Streep does it when no one's looking.

Phyllis George pumps iron. So does Linda Johnson Robb—her momma taught her how.

Joni Mitchell, Judy Collins, Joan Baez are all Real Women. Melissa Manchester used to be. ✦

Sandra Day O'Connor did it for a while. Then she decided it might hurt her chances for immortality. The muscle definition still shows.

Diana Nyad does it to death.

Diana Ross and the Supremes were Real Women. Diana gone solo is an iron pumper except when Lionel Ritchie talks her out of it.

Anne Gorsuch is an iron-pumper. Elizabeth Dole is not.

Abigail Van Buren pumps, but Ann Landers probably doesn't. Lynn Redgrave is an occasional pumper, Vanessa never.

All Miss Texas contestants for Miss America pump iron.

Anita Bryant pumps but she keeps it in the closet. Marie Osmond pumps with the whole family. So does Debby Boone.

Gilda Radner was a Real Woman, until she took up with Gene Wilder, who is definitely not a Real Man. Same thing happened to Marsha Mason, for whom all was Real until the marriage to Neil Simon.

Doris Day is a Real Woman; Debbie Reynolds has been pumping ever since Eddie & Liz.

Unfortunately, the entire British Empire seems seriously threatened by the wayward habit. After all, they are led by a Prime Minister whose nickname is "Iron Lady."

"*I wish I had watched Falcon Crest
instead of Private Benjamin.*"

Real Women

Bette Davis
Jacqueline Kennedy Onassis
Jean Harris
Diana, Princess of Wales
Loretta Lynn
Millicent Fenwick
Lily Tomlin
Julia Child
Karen Silkwood
Billie Jean King
Joan of Arc
Eleanor Roosevelt
Isadora Duncan
Margaret Mead
Aretha Franklin
Mary Tyler Moore
Hannah Arendt
Cyd Charisse
Pallas Athena
Ellen Burstyn
Glenda Jackson
Rock Hudson
Alice Roosevelt Longworth
Elizabeth Taylor*

*No matter how fat she gets, no matter how many times
she marries Richard Burton, no matter how many tur-
keys she stars in.

Iron Pumpers

Nancy Reagan
Jeane Kirkpatrick
Mother Teresa
Queen Elizabeth II
Sue Mengers
Dr. Joyce Brothers
Phyllis Schlafly
Lina Wertmuller

Evita Perón
Indira Gandhi
Gloria Vanderbilt
Anita Bryant
Arlene Dahl
Cheryl Tiegs
Jeane Dixon

Fakers and Phonies

Bianca Jagger
Mick Jagger
Diana Vreeland
Olivia Newton-John
Zsa Zsa Gabor

Brooke Shields
Miss Divine
Muffy Brandon
Marabel Morgan
Bo Derek

Today's Real Woman

What's a girl to do? Sexual liberation was supposed to be for women, not San Francisco.

Modern times are truly here. Not only is today's woman supposed to have the kids, make them dinner at night, and put them through college, but smile when she gets introduced to her husband's new boyfriend.

Men, as usual, are trying to co-opt all available kvetch time. Now they're feeling sexually used, wondering about the reality of the commitment, having mid-life crises, and reading books on how to be "real."

How does today's Real Woman keep her balance? How does she deal with managing corporate takeovers during the day and forgetting what I. Q. stands for at night?

Post-pill, post-gay rights, post-Gloria Steinem and buddy movies and Consciousness Raising, after the rehabilitation of Jane Fonda *and* Richard Nixon *and* the mini-skirt, how does the Real Woman stay alive? How does she chew up the competition into little pieces, spit it out, grind the remains beneath her high heel and still remain a lady?

With style, of course.

Now that things like white gloves, tea dances, and headaches before bed have gone the way of the American automobile industry, the options for ladylike behavior are subtle to the point of evaporation. But they do exist. It is possible for the Real Woman to separate herself from the burgeoning flocks of flagrant imitators even when the lingerie department of Lord & Taylor's is no longer for women only. She can establish herself as the real thing without losing either her performance bonus or her hairdresser to less dignified competitors.

For one thing, the Real Woman is a generous tipper—her manicurist knows better than to try defecting.

Real Women believe palimony was invented by some headline-grabbing lawyer to serve his own greedy ends. They feel sorry for Vicky Morgan and Michelle Triola, but think those girls should have known better. They also think Jean Harris should have been acquitted.

Real Women don't ask if the sex was good. They know it was.

Real Women have their hair tinted or hennaed, never dyed.

Real Women try to keep that heart-of-gold image when they can. They seek out ways to show they are still the kind, caring people they were before Kate Millet's karate kick.

Real Women give at the office.

Real Women still pass their share of the dinner tab under the table when anyone else—like the maitre d' or in-laws—is around.

Real Women are genuinely concerned about the environment, nuclear disarmament, baby seals. They are not concerned about the capabilities of the F 1-11 fighter plane or the future of baseball.

Real Women like cute things. They can't help themselves. Teddy bears, newborn kittens, Richard Gere always inspire coos.

In spite of everything, Real Women continue to adhere to traditional feminine values. Within reason.

Real Women let men open doors, light cigarettes, pull out chairs. They do not let men invest their money or drive their cars.

Real Women cry at the movies. A lot. They also cry at the evening news, airports, and upon the engagement of their best friends.

Real Women think it's a nice idea for the men to share in the housework. If only it wasn't one more thing she has to pretend he can do right.

Real Women use perfumed bath soaps and put sachets in the linen closet. They also own a bottle of Chanel #5 bought after raking in the first million. ✦

Real Women do not smoke long brown cigarettes. They do not smoke Virginia Slims or Eves.

Real Women do not have visible panty lines.

Real Women always have the sales receipt.

Real Women try to make things as pleasant as possible for other people. They use ZIP codes, exact change, tie-top garbage bags. Real Women floss.

Real Women do not have anxiety attacks.

Real Women do not call other women "broads."

Real Women never turn down World Series tickets.

Politically, the Real Woman believes in moderation. She is not registered as a member of any party, although she always votes. On every proposition and every race. She also knows that—unfortunate but true—reforming zealots are social bores while corrupt fatcats are genial and charming.

Real Women support the ERA. They also support the death penalty if Phyllis Schlafly is the first to go.

Real Women don't worry about money in any form except cash.

Real Women know that Jimmy Connors and Pete Rose are the same person.

Real Women do not drink fuzzy drinks like pink squirrels or strawberry daiquiris. They drink hard liquor straight only after totaling the car. Or a romance. They take white wine intravenously. They never drink beer in quart bottles, never an entire sixpack by themselves. National brands only. Real Women are cocktail drinkers: gin and tonic, vodka gimlets, Scotch and soda.

Real Women wish they would run into Philip Marlowe or a reasonable facsimile thereof in the very near future.

Real Women are good dancers. They are also charitable dancers. They always make the man look at least competent.

Real Women use Crest.

Real Women are a little tired of Pac-Man. They are more than a little tired of home video games, but this does not mean they can't whip any man's ass.

Real Women don't understand the fuss about Vince Lombardi—wasn't he just a hard-nosed coach from a little burg in Wisconsin?

Real Women do not believe the psychological phase labeled "penis envy" ever existed.

Real Women do not believe diamonds are forever. But they're a good down payment.

Real Women do not believe that Joan Crawford did all those things to Christina.

Real Women hate the phrase "Boys will be boys."

Real Women do not buy beefcake calendars. They see enough of the real thing.

Real Women know perfectly well that keeping in shape is a good idea. They exercise regularly, but not by rolling on the floor with Richard Simmons on the T. V.

Real Women can and do work out with weights when the spirit moves them. They are not as compulsive about body-building as men because they have better bodies to begin with. What they will never do is use lame-brained macho jargon like "Pump Iron" to describe their work with weights. Real Women know that the macho mentality, not the men themselves, is the real enemy. Men, on the other hand, seem to have developed the absurd notion that quiche is their enemy.

Real Women know better. Real Women know that when men try quiche, they will like it.

Or else.

Real Woman Q & A

Q. Which of the following would a Real Woman rather do?

1. Squash a big spider
2. Shoo away a garter snake
3. Dissect a frog
4. Find a leech on her leg
5. Face a firing squad

A. .... Don't rush her! ... She's *thinking*.

What Real Women Really Want

A self-appointed pundit of machismo has recently tried to revive a mummified macho mystique as archaic as the Code Duello, the Double Standard, the Unwritten Law. In so doing, he has divided all males into one of two distinct camps: the Wimps who are good for nothing but talk, talk, talk, and the Machos, who settle all disputes with a flamethrower. This sort of narrow mentality might try to divide all Womankind into two separate groups, the Passive Pussycats and the Pushy Bitches. Real Women are too sharp for that.

Real Women know they can be more delicate than Audrey Hepburn or more robust than Billie Jean King, yet still be feminine. Real Women know they can be more reactionary than Phyllis Schlafly or more radical than Jane Fonda yet still be feminine. Real Women know they can be more ladylike than Nancy Reagan or more butch than Gertrude Stein, yet still be feminine. Real Women have proof of this, and her name is Katharine Hepburn.

Real Women are not ambivalent about their femininity. They accept their natural superiority with easy grace, not feeling any compulsion to drum other women out of the corps for imagined offenses against some outdated code.

Real Women do not ask for much—only to have it both ways, always. ✦

Five Things The Real Woman May Have to Fake

1. Interest in professional football.

2. Remembering an old boyfriend.

3. Not remembering an old boyfriend.

4. Orgasm.

5. Youth.

Five Things The Real Woman Never Fakes

1. **Her diamonds.**

2. **Her bust.**

3. **Her accent.**

4. **Her furs.**

5. **Her Ph.D.s**

"I, too, gave up my career as a prima ballerina for a greater love—chocolate."

★ THE
★ REAL
★ WOMAN
★ TRADITION

A Real Woman of Yesteryear

The most brilliant man in the world was Peter Abelard, a clergyman in Paris. The most beautiful and accomplished woman was his teenage pupil, Héloise. A forbidden passion engulfed them. When the scandal became public, her uncle, Canon Fulbert, felt humiliated enough to hire ruffians to castrate Abelard. Even for the 12th century, this was a pretty nasty piece of business.

A lesser woman, a woman of another sort, a false woman, might have been tempted to fall in love with another man (one still anatomically intact, for instance), but not Héloise. Héloise was a Real Woman's Real Woman. She took the veil, entered a nunnery, became Abbess of the Paraclete and devoted her last 45 years to writing love letters to Abelard, even though he had, perhaps understandably but ungallantly all the same, cooled toward her. Thus the world's greatest love letters, full of fiery passion and selfless devotion, were written by a nun to an emasculated theologian. ✶

Dates The Real Woman Prefers To Forget

31 BC
Cleopatra commits suicide
when she learns that her
beloved Marc Antony is
dead. A Real Woman ought
to give her all for love,
but not by baring her
bosom to a poisonous snake.
Ugh!

1431
Joan of Arc is burned
at the stake for
showing up the men
at their own game.

1491
Birth of Henry VIII,
who set *such* a bad
example for husbands
everywhere.

1692
Women in Salem,
Massachusetts, practice
witchcraft, giving all
womankind a bad name.

1937
Amelia Earhart lost
over the Pacific.

1950
First televised NFL game.

1982
*Real Men Don't
Eat Quiche*
published.

Highlights of Real Woman's Past

DAY ONE
Eve persuades Adam
that he has no hope
of promotion in The
Garden of Eden,
becoming the first
"Woman Behind the Man."

1210 BC
Clytemnestra cuts the
throat of her husband
because Agamemnon came
home late from work ... ten
years late.

SOMEWHAT LATER
Delilah proves that beauty
and brains can outmatch brawn.

419 BC
Xanthippe nags Socrates.
If she hadn't the lazy
bum might have remained
a village layabout.

59 BC
A resourceful Roman matron
invents indoor plumbing to
the relief of everyone,
except a few males foolhardy
enough to keep going outside
in below zero weather.

799

Charlemagne takes his first
bite of quiche, prepared by
his wife Blanchefleur, and
pronounces it delicious.

965

The Double Standard suffers
a major setback when Pope Leo VIII
dies while committing adultery.

1088

Lady Macbeth inspires her
husband to improve their
social standing.

1140

Romantic Love is invented
and popularized by Eleanor
of Aquitaine and her
troubadours.

1221

Alison Bath, wife of a
Crusader, learns to pick
the lock on her chastity
belt and becomes the first
truly liberated woman.

1492

Isabella I of Spain takes pity
on a poor sailor and gives him
the wherewithal to discover
the New World.

1588

Elizabeth I
shows up the
macho Philip II by
defeating
his Armada.

1609

Pocahontas saves Captain John
Smith, not to mention the entire
Virginia Colony, from extinction.

1745

Madame de Pompadour creates
an uplifting hairstyle, thereby
forestalling the French Revolution
for more than 40 years.

1776

Martha Washington
keeps George's
entire army from
freezing at
Valley Forge.

1818

Mary Shelley gives her
poet-husband his due in
her autobiographical novel,
Frankenstein.

1837

Queen Victoria ascends to the
British throne, inaugurating the
great era of Real Womanhood.

1850

First French perfumes
appear on the market.

1876

Tired of waiting for her
ne'er-do-well son, Alexander
Graham, to make something of
himself, Ma Bell invents the
telephone.

1900

Carrie Nation makes more than
a few Real Men wish that hard
liquor had never been invented.

1920

The Nineteenth Amendment
is passed.

1943-45

Rosie the Riveter demonstrates
what a woman can do when
given a chance and a few
power tools of her own.

1963

Invention of the
birth control pill.

1974

Billie Jean King
beats Bobby Riggs.

1975

Elizabeth Taylor
marries
Richard Burton
for love . . . again.

1979

After years of Hatties, Hildas,
Betseys, and Beulahs, a hurricane
is finally named David.

1980

JR is finally shot.

1981

Lady Diana marries
Prince Charles.

1982

Publication of
*Real Women
Never Pump Iron.*

"I know I did, and I plan to keep doing it
until they restore full service."

★ REAL
★ WOMEN
★ ON
★ THE
★ MOVE

The Real Woman Behind the Wheel

If there's one thing the Real Woman hates, it's jokes about women drivers. They make her so mad she wants to run somebody over.

She tries to be a careful driver, a courteous driver, a considerate driver. She pays tolls, never tailgates, brakes for animals and trucks. She observes the 55-mile-per-hour speed limit, at least when she also observes a police car.

When other people are not as careful as she is, she loses her temper. Shortly thereafter, she may lose control. In fact, it is behind the wheel of a car that the Real Woman reaches her finest hour as verbal abuser of her fellow man. Like her mother before her—at whose side she first learned this skill—the Real Woman finds another car's least infraction against driving protocol the perfect occasion to display her technique in invective, insult and defamation of character. The hours and days of confining herself to "darn it" and "oh, fudge" when in mixed company are finally avenged. For the Real Woman, that drive to the mall has the potential for being a truly cathartic experience.

Gone are the days, of course, when the back seat of a Ford was a place of mystery and romance. Cars have become smaller, mores less restrictive—the more prosaic bed is the modern young lovers' battlefield. There's no telling, however, when emergency measures may become necessary. For this reason, Real Women continue to appreciate the spacious accommodations provided by Lee Iacocca and his forebears. She herself may not be able to afford a gas-guzzling monster from Detroit, but she sure as hell hopes her boyfriend can.

Other behavioral characteristics of the Real Woman behind the wheel:

Real Women do not customize their automobiles. They do not install computerized horns that play "Dixie." They do not install glass packs or air shocks. They fix their mufflers right away. They do not want a car that draws attention to itself. Unless that car is a fire-engine-red Maserati or a sky-blue Mercedes sedan with power everything.

Real Women do not enter Demolition Derbies. They don't drag race. They don't play chicken. They don't peel rubber pulling out of driveways.

Real Women do flirt with gas station attendants. The cute ones, that is. There is an ineffable appeal here that also attaches itself to construction workers, lifeguards, firefighters and all men wearing a uniform of any sort whatsoever.

Real Women grew up in families with real brothers. Many Real Women are excellent mechanics who can tear down and rebuild an engine. They know, however, that mechanics resent women interfering in their field of expertise. So they play dumb. Initially. But if the mechanic tries to pad the bill with so much as an extra cotter pin, the Real Woman reads him the riot act.

Real Women do not change flat tires. (They know how, they refuse on principle.) Real Women also do not check their own oil. They prefer not to touch something called a "dipstick."

Real Women don't drive getaway cars. Unless, that is, they are getting the same cut on the job as everyone else.

Real Women do not own funny cars. Triple whites, denim interiors, roll bars, tear drop windows are not welcome. The Gucci Cadillac is the Real Woman's idea of gross. No vanity plates, no carpeting on the dash, no graduation tassel hanging from the rearview. A small mirror on the upside of the driver's sun visor is permissible.

Real Women buckle their seat belts. Except when they are wearing a linen suit fresh from the cleaner's.

Real Women drive stick shifts. Fuel economy aside, they're more fun. But they can also maneuver a Chrysler Imperial through the narrowest of double-parked city streets without so much as a break in the conversation. ✦

The Real Woman and her Career

Real Women with MBAs from Harvard are no longer content with the only job that used to be available to them—that of Avon lady.

No: the challenge confronting Real Women in today's real world is breaking the bondage of stereotypes to enter the lucrative male-dominated careers where the real action is. If you put a Real Woman in the steno pool today, she'll be Director of Marketing by the end of the year en route to the corporate boardroom and bedroom by 1984. ✶

Six Careers The Real Woman Shuns

★★★★★★★★★★★★★★★★★★★★★★★★★★★★

1.   Mud Wrestler

2.   Masseuse

3.   Bouncer

4.   Loan Shark

5.   Oil Rig Roughneck

6.   Carnival Barker

Real Woman's Profile

Pamela Wheelwright

BORN: Peoria, Illinois, 1947

HOME: Chevy Chase, Maryland

OCCUPATIONS: Justice, U. S. Supreme Court; Owner, NFL Team; President of Production, 20th Century Limited; Editor-in-Chief, *Cosmopolitan Magazine*; Vice-President of Promotion, Bendex Corp.; Headmistress, The Bellevoir School, Charlottesville, Virginia; cosmetics tycoon, Dallas, Texas.

BIGGEST ACCOMPLISHMENTS: As first woman Justice, made landmark decisions on sexual harassment in workplace, palimony; as first woman owner of pro football team, traded away All-Pro linebackers for sleek young wide receivers (although this did not help the club's standing, it did help my standing at the country club); became first woman studio head after successful modeling career; quadrupled circulation of foundering woman's magazine by focusing on real world issues like sex for singles, making it on your own in a man's world, trendy cosmetics; after extraordinarily rapid rise to power in Bendex Corp., resigned to marry Chairman of the Board; became youngest headmistress in history of century-old finishing school (agreed to leave after shooting mishap); as Marketing Director for Texas cosmetics firm, trebled sales, devised concept of pink Cadillac for top saleswomen.

HOBBIES: Golf, hang-gliding. Passionate Alpinist, first climbed Matterhorn at 14. Charter member of the Putney, Vermont, chapter of the Elvis Presley Fan Club. Volunteer fund-raiser for NOW.

LAST BOOK READ: *101 Quiche Recipes.*

PERSONALITY SKETCH: Attractive, dynamic, rich, totally feminine.

SCOTCH: The best. Straight on imported rocks.

QUOTE: "I did it all my way."

*"I do wish my George had pectorals like that . . .
to speak only of pectorals."*

★ THE
★ CULTIVATED
★ REAL
★ WOMAN

Reading and The Real Woman

Women are the real readers in America. They are the mainstay of American publishing, and the last bastion of literacy. Because of their overwhelming significance, Real Women are the prime market for many distasteful or at least tasteless book and magazine products. Without even trying, the Real Woman can easily find herself knee-deep in verbal kitsch. She is forced by the onslaught of coy advertising to pick her way through the literary landscape with great care.

Real Women do not read novelizations. They read novels. Real Women have read *Gone With the Wind* five times.

Real Women read film stars' autobiographies. By the truckload. Lana, Ingrid, Betty, Shelley—they want to know all about it. In detail, please.

Real Women do not own *The Joy of Sex*. They get the general idea checking out a (male) friend's copy. In fact, Real Women eschew sex manuals altogether, even if they do think it's sweet that Masters & Johnson are married.

Real Women do own, and have reason from time to time to consult, helpful volumes like *Three Contributions to the Theory of Sexuality* and *Inhibitions, Symptoms and Anxiety*. The Real Woman knows that Sigmund Freud has the Real Man's number.

Real Women like to nibble on a nice, big, fat, Gothic romance. They do not read nurse novels or stewardess novels.

Real Women read classics by other Real Women. Jane Austen is a special favorite. Virginia Woolf, of course. Colette. Charlotte Bronte. Real Women do not care for Ayn Rand.

Magazines. Magazines were invented for the Real Woman. Glossy paper does something special for her. But, once again, care must be taken to avoid the quagmire of kitsch. In general, the Real Woman finds that a balanced, tit-for-tat approach is the best subscription policy. *MS.* is okay if you're also getting the *MLA Journal. The New Yorker* if you get *People,* too. It's fine to subscribe to *Redbook* or *Ladies Home Journal* (for "Can This Marriage Be Saved?" if nothing else) if you're also getting *Esquire.* Furthermore:

Real Women buy *Glamour* and *Vogue* and *Mademoiselle* off the newsstand with some regularity. They can keep up with the other women's mags in the dentist's office.

Real Women never buy any publication with a centerfold.

Real Women read fanzines and lurid tabloids but never buy them. They know that grocery store check-out lines are for *The National Enquirer.*

Real Women know that it's important to keep up with what's *really* happening in today's world. For this purpose they do not read *Time, Newsweek, New Republic,* or *U. S. News and World Report.* They read *Sports Illustrated.*

Real Women look at *G. Q.* This is reconnaissance work. The Real Woman considers her boyfriend's and her boss's wardrobe her business.

Real Women do not look at *Mad Magazine* or *National Lampoon.* They know that, no matter what anyone says, these publications fall into the category also occupied by setting ants on fire with magnifying glasses, putting cats in clothes dryers and racing dirt bikes—fun for boys only.

Five Fictional Heroes That Have Spoiled Real Men for Real Women

1. **Heathcliff in *Wuthering Heights.***

2. **Count Vronsky in *Anna Karenina.***

3. **Fitzwilliam Darcy in *Pride and Prejudice.***

4. **Benedick in *Much Ado About Nothing.***

5. **Mr. Rochester in *Jane Eyre.***

Real Woman Q & A

★★★★★★★★★★★★★★★

Q. What does the Real Woman do when she comes home unexpectedly and catches her husband in bed with her best friend?

1. Forgive him for the sake of the children and blame the other woman completely.

2. Call the best divorce lawyer in the state.

A. Both. The Real Woman will keep her options open until that sharp lawyer finds out exactly how good a settlement she can expect.

The Real Woman's TV Viewing

Real Women know that television is made especially for them. They also know that there are very few Real Women actually on T. V. This allows them to think, all protesting aside, that television programming is a product of the ever devious Real Male Mind. *Charlie's Angels,* for instance. Remember that one? Big-time iron-pumpers camouflaged as Real Women and you're supposed to sit blankfaced while the man of the house lurches between laughter and leers. Whatever happened to nice ladies in crisp skirts with a sense of self respect like Della Street on *Perry Mason*? She never wore halter tops or hotpants on the job.

Real Women like it better when *everyone* acts dumb. This is part of the reason they like soap operas. In the afternoon—or in disguise as prime-time shows like *Knots Landing* or *Flamingo Road*—Real Women like seeing men reduced to the same level of banal but always emotionally charged dialogue that women have had put in their mouths for years. Anyway, where else do you get to hear men talk about their love lives in the intense tones usually reserved for the NFL?

On soap operas the iron-pumpers are fully acknowledged and out in the open. Love-to-hate ladies like Erica Kane on *All My Children* or the Joan Collins character on *Dynasty* are T. V.'s best entertainment value.

Real Women really wish loud, unattractive, unfunny iron-pumpers like Lucille Ball and Linda Lavin were not such big hits. It's almost more insulting than the blondes in hotpants. It is excruciatingly painful for the Real Woman to watch *Alice* or Lucy in any of her incarnations.

Real Women ask this question: Couldn't all three major networks do all the football on one day and get it over with?

Real Women protest sex and violence on television. But it's not the kids they're worried about. Kids have common sense. Kids have minds of their own. Kids can distinguish fantasy from reality. Real Women have found that Real Men do not exhibit similar powers of discrimination.

Real Women like Jessica Savitch, don't like Jane Pauley. Jessica does her job. She doesn't flirt with other anchor persons, she doesn't wear ribbons in her hair, she doesn't grin after giving the kill count in Lebanon. Real Women feel sorry for Garry Trudeau, and wonder if it isn't Jane's fault he decided to stop drawing *Doonesbury* for a while, poor dear. Diane Sawyer they take a wait-and-see attitude on, she could go either way.

Real Women always watch the Academy Awards. Always.

Real Women know that *Mary Tyler Moore* was the funniest show ever. It is the log they cling to in the sea of bad T. V.

Real Women like Johnny Carson. Most of their children owe Mr. Carson their existence. They especially like Johnny for introducing them to Joan Rivers, who is always funnier than any of the male comedians.

Some further Real Women likes and dislikes:

★★★★★★★★★★★★★★★★★★★★★★★★★

General Hospital. Love and death in the afternoon.	*Shuttle lift-offs.* Especially when the landing is covered live in the middle of *General Hospital.*
Phil Donahue. Extra credit for Marlo.	*Merv Griffin.* If he says "great gal" one more time . . . .
MacNeil-Lehrer. Two cute, smart guys and it's only half an hour, how can you lose?	*Family Feud.* Is there anything Richard Dawson won't kiss?
Masterpiece Theatre. Triple treat. Cute guys in soap operas with English accents.	*Monday Night Football.* Saturday and Sunday wasn't enough, right?
Taxi. Marilu Henner holds her own, no hotpants.	*Three's Company.* Corny, horny, and smarmy.
Sixty Minutes. Mike Wallace is adorable, and Andy Rooney is macho.	*Real People.* Real idiots.
Wide World of Sports. To show she's not anti-sport, just anti-football.	*Thursday Night Football.* No comment.
Honeymooners reruns. Alice definitely has the right idea.	*I Dream of Jeannie reruns.* Even J. R. was a wimp in this one.
Tom Brokaw. T. V.'s #1 man. And so clever.	*Bob Hope Specials.* Still trying to prove he can tell a girl from a boy. That's good, Bob. Really interesting.

The Real Woman at the Movies

Real Women adore movies. They know that image is more important than mere reality. They understand that life copies art and that in America, the only art form that really matters is movies. Although variations exist, there are certain standard prejudices shared by all movie-going Real Women.

When it comes to stars, male stars, Real Women agree that Cary Grant can do no wrong. Lee Marvin, Lee Majors, and Lee Van Cleef are, on the other hand, always wrong. James Dean is universally worshipped, especially in *East of Eden*. Woody Allen is thought to be awfully cute, but Real Women do wish guys would stop cribbing his lines. Real Women will go to see James Bond movies when 007 is played by Sean Connery only. Sorry, Roger. Sean is undressed through most of *Thunderball* and with good reason.

Real Women will see reruns of Grace Kelly in anything and everything. They admire Mae West—they wish they could get away with it, they know she wrote her own scripts. Marilyn Monroe they see as a victim. They wish she'd stop trying so hard. (The same goes for Judy Garland.) But it is for the ladies with the steely voices and "get lost, buddy" sex appeal that they reserve their greatest love—Bette Davis, Barbara Stanwyck, Ida Lupino are the Real Woman's real screen heroines. ✦

Real Women try to like Westerns. War movies are out of the question. *The Best Years of Our Lives, The Men, Coming Home*—Real Women don't mind weeping over guys who have already been shot to bits, but they get no kick out of watching the imbeciles do it.

Real Women avoid Sam Peckinpah movies, unless the only alternative is Russ Meyer. (Under duress they will concede that *Beyond the Valley of the Dolls* is a very funny picture—Meyer is gross, but he's also fair—all sexes look equally silly.)

Further movie-going preferences:

Real Women have seen all seven Fred & Ginger pictures a minimum of seven times each.

Real Women have seen one (1) porno movie. Usually *Deep Throat*—at least it's a classic.

Real Women are not Miss Prisses. Discreet necking is what movies were invented for. However, making noises and undoing clothing is going too far—Real Women always want to see the whole picture, from beginning to end, no interruptions, please. That's why Real Men fetch the popcorn and soda.

Real Women go to foreign movies with their girlfriends or a guy they are trying to ditch.

Real Women go to horror movies with a guy they are not trying to ditch.

The Real Woman's Favorite Films

Gone With the Wind
Some Like It Hot
Bringing Up Baby
How to Marry a
  Millionaire
Diamonds Are Forever
Casablanca
Dark Victory
Singin' in the Rain
The Swan
Chinatown
A Streetcar Named Desire
Hud
Butch Cassidy and the
  Sundance Kid (Twice)
Wuthering Heights
Once Is Not Enough
My Fair Lady
Bullitt
Romeo and Juliet
Tom Jones
West Side Story

Cat on a Hot Tin Roof
Adam's Rib
Sabrina
A Place in the Sun
Born Yesterday
Annie Hall
Julia
Alice Doesn't Live
  Here Anymore
The Go-Between
Notorious
The Miracle Worker
Two for the Road
No Way to Treat a Lady
Personal Best
Mrs. Miniver
The Little Foxes
The Lady Eve
Nine to Five
My Brilliant Career
I'm No Angel

Ten Films The Real Woman Wouldn't Pay to See

1. Death Wish

2. Road Warrior

3. Cruising

4. Night of the Blood Beast

5. The Longest Yard

6. Magnum Force*

7. Scarecrow

8. Raging Bull

9. Tora! Tora! Tora!

10. Mother, Jugs & Speed

*Or any other Clint Eastwood movie.

"Let's just put a smaller number on the inside."

The Real Woman's Listening Pleasure

The Real Woman likes music. She likes records. She likes to listen to the radio. She does not, however, like stereo systems. She does not know anything about them. Generally, she owns an indifferent assortment of receiver, speakers, and turntable, the needle of which has never been changed. Big deal sound systems with lots of component parts, and dials, and lights, and switches for every conceivable operation are strictly for the boys.

The Real Woman does not take very good care of her records. She does not clean them, store them properly, categorize them by artist or label or in any other way exhibit fetishistic tendencies. Scratchy, dusty, battered records, some without sleeves or jackets, are the order of the Real Woman's collection. Some records are worn beyond playing—these records represent important moments in the Real Woman's life, for the most part important romantic moments.

Real Women do have a profound weakness for love songs, particularly love songs by male vocalists. This does not translate into a profound weakness for Barry Manilow, whom the Real Woman could definitely live without.

Real Women like to hear love songs from Frank Sinatra (of course), Paul McCartney, Sam Cooke, Buddy Holly, James Ingram, George Jones, Luther Vandross and Hank Williams. As far as the Real Woman is concerned the greatest love song writers are Cole Porter, Hoagy "Stardust" Carmichael, John Lennon and Messrs. Holland/Dozier/Holland.

Real Women don't talk about it, but they believe Tom Jones and Engelbert Humperdinck and Steve Lawrence are great singers. They like Elvis best when he sounds like one of these three, even though they understand this was not the sound that made Elvis famous.

Real Women do not own records by Pink Floyd, Black Sabbath (that Ozzie Osborn is *disgusting*), the Allman Brothers, REO Speedwagon, The Who. Never have, never will. They may have attended concerts by these performers under pressure from a (former) boyfriend who paid for the ticket.

Real Women adore Bonnie Raitt. They have all her records. They like Laura Nyro and Carol King, although as writers rather than recording artists. Linda Ronstadt is considered too cute for her own good.

Real Women think Frank Zappa is gross.

Real Women do not get Patti Smith. She is a girl for guys. Maybe she is a guy. The same goes for Rickie Lee Jones.

Real Women have a special place in their hearts and their record collections for all-girl groups—good, bad, or indifferent. They have everything on vinyl by the Go-Gos, the Shirelles, the Ronettes, Joy of Cooking, the Runaways.

Real Women love the Stones and have all their albums until *Some Girls*, when they started repeating themselves.

Real Women have spent their formative years deeply envious of lead singers like Grace Slick, Chrissie Hynde, Gladys Knight—women who made it as one of the guys.

Janis Joplin is the Real Woman's numero uno. Cher should be ashamed to be alive in the same century.

Lena Horne is a Real Woman. Eydie Gorme works out like a fiend. Karen Carpenter is also an iron-pumper, even if she has been giving her do-nothing brother a free ride all these years. Tammi Terrell is a Real Woman. Martha Reeves is a Real Woman. In fact, most Motown Recording Artists (including Michael Jackson) are Real Women.

Real Women do not know much about the great divas—Joan Sutherland, Birgit Nilsson, Montserrat Caballe—but they suspect iron pumping. The big exception is Maria Callas, who instantly rates for losing all that weight and having a tempestuous affair with a Greek shipping magnate. Beverly Sills is likable enough, but can you really extend Real Woman status to a person whose nickname is Bubbles?

"I warned you about rushing the net."

★ THE
★ PHYSICAL
★ REAL
★ WOMAN

The Real Woman Athlete

Sports are still a proving ground of Real Womanhood. In some cases, the Real Woman sticks to the traditional (British) definitions—she will play croquet, for instance, but not cricket. Field hockey, yes; ice hockey, no. Other times she plays to look good—sports that require specific clothing like golf and skiing particularly appeal to the Real Woman. The hammer throw, for a similar reason, does not. Mostly, she plays to win and look good doing it. Thus, racquet sports are at the top of the Real Woman's sporting list. She excels at squash, badminton, racquetball, tennis.

Especially tennis. Real Women have great backhand volleys, but they do not work on the power game. Aside from those darling little outfits, tennis is a game the Real Woman plays in the belief that even Real Men need to be challenged at the net. When Real Women protest an especially bad call by the head linesman, they do not shout obscenities ... they mutter them in a stage whisper.

Real Women are not sissies. They can bag game and clean fish. They'd just rather not if there is any conceivable way to get out of it.

Real Women do not throw like girls.

Real Women do not win black belts in karate. They don't like the idea of registering parts of their anatomy with the police.

Real Women do not take steroids.

Real Women do not cry real tears when they beat a doubles partner in three sets in the quarterfinals of a Grand Slam tennis tournament.

Real Women take jacks seriously. Hopscotch, too.

Real Women swim beautifully, but resent jokes about the breast stroke. (Swimming goes against the clothing-specific grain. When the Real Woman goes swimming she wears a Speedo.)

Real Women who bowl bring their own shoes.

Real Women never remember the score.

Real Women compete in the high jump, but not in the high hurdles.

Real Women love to body surf, but never in a bikini.

Real Women jog, but do not run in marathons.

Real Women ice skate with some persistence, always hoping to be transformed into Peggy Fleming or Dorothy Hamill when they hit the ice.

Real Women will take up archery. They will not take up darts.

Real Women know better than to bother beating men at pool or ping-pong.

Real Women eschew rugby. And football (except touch at the Kennedy compound), volleyball (death to long, red fingernails), handball, basketball (Real Women never slam-dunk *anything*), and softball (unless it's slo-pitch at a charity picnic).

Real Women play Scrabble brilliantly, but always let Real Men win at Monopoly. ✦

The Real Woman in the Locker Room

Real Women do not have any special brand of chatter for the Women's Locker Room. They talk about clothes, diets, men, the weather, just about everything except sports.

Real Women journalists whose work takes them into Men's Locker Rooms should never gasp and say "Oh wow!"

Real Women wonder why, if women journalists are allowed in Men's Locker Rooms, men journalists are not allowed in Women's Locker Rooms. A Real Woman might have reservations about John Madden or Howard Cosell, but Tom Seaver or John Brodie serve the cause of equal rights very well. ✦

The Real Woman and Food

The Real Woman tries to keep her diet to herself. And her best friend. She *never* lets men know she gives a second thought to pizza with extra cheese or chocolate cake with chocolate frosting. It's a question of pride, of maintaining that aura of effortless perfection so crucial to her image.

This does not mean that the Real Woman doesn't worry about what she eats. She does, all the time. How can she help it when prepubescent teen models are the going thing in sex symbols and losing weight is the nation's leading growth industry? It's an article of faith that every new diet book is dutifully bought and read, every new plan tried for one week, or until boredom and starvation set in, whichever comes first.

For all the hoopla, dieting is much more a subject for conversation than concern. Actual weight loss is largely a vaguely longed for by-product of what is really an elaborate system of communication. Diets are the great common ground of Real Womanhood. They have replaced babies and soap operas as the topics of choice conversation on streetcorners, in elevators, over kitchen tables and along grocery store aisles across the land. It's the way Real Women greet each other, show concern, pay compliments, issue insults, establish bonds, judge character.

Being nice is telling someone she looks skinnier. Much skinnier. Sharing diet secrets means you're well on the road to being best friends. Is someone eating raw lettuce morning, noon and night? The Real Woman is sympathetic but would never consult that someone on a serious business matter. Has someone stopped having a bagel and cream cheese with her morning cup of coffee? Time to make discreet inquiries into that someone's lovelife.

Passing acquaintance with the basics of all major diets is de rigueur. Every self-respecting Real Woman knows that a half grapefruit for breakfast and cold cuts for dinner is Scarsdale, eight glasses of water a day is Stillman, pineapples till you turn into one is Beverly Hills, and so on. This is crucial social information and ignorance indicates iron-pumping tendencies.

The Real Woman's Two-Day Diet Plan

DAY 1: GLUTTONY
Crème de Menthe Parfait
Banana Split
Strawberry Shortcake
Chocolate-Covered Cherries
Lemon Meringue Pie
Blueberry Cheesecake

DAY 2: REMORSE
Wheat Thins
Cucumber Slices
Ex-Lax
Cigarettes
Bouillon
Ayds
Watercress
Dexatrim
Celery Stalks
Carrot Sticks
D-Zerta Diet Gelatine

"I can't believe I ate the whole thing."

Real Woman's Quiche Recipe

1. Line a 9-inch pie pan with pastry dough.

2. Prick sides and bottom of pastry and bake in a preheated 450° oven for 5 minutes.

3. Fry 4 strips bacon until crisp and remove from the skillet. Pour off all but 1 tablespoon of the fat, and in it cook 1 thinly sliced onion until the onion is transparent.

4. Crumble the bacon, and spread it, the onion, and 1 cup cubed Swiss cheese in the bottom of the cooled pie shell.

5. Combine 3 slightly beaten eggs, 1½ cups half-and-half, ¼ teaspoon nutmeg, ⅛ teaspoon cayenne pepper, ½ teaspoon salt, and strain over the cheese-bacon-onion mixture.

6. Bake at 450° for 15 minutes and then reduce the heat to 350° and bake 10-15 minutes longer or until the custard sets.

Serves three hungry Real Men.

The Real Woman in the Kitchen

The Real Woman always bakes from scratch. She would never use a mix. She does keep Stouffer's frozen food line in the freezer for emergencies. The Real Woman does not consider taking credit for thawing an actual *lie*. Real Women are allowed to fudge with the facts when it comes to their age, their past, and their cooking.

The Real Woman never shares a recipe.

The Real Woman always uses fresh produce.

A Real Woman demands a "self-cleaning oven." She tells herself that the self-cleaning oven really is cleaning itself, just as she tells herself that her husband is faithful. The Real Woman never investigates, for fear she may find herself cleaning an oven.

A Real Woman whose stove does not have an oven that claims to clean itself learns to squint when the kitchen fills with smoke.

A Real Woman knows two things: (1) what her kid ought to eat; and (2) what her kid will eat. Therefore, she always puts a Hostess Twinkie in the lunchbox alongside a granola bar.

The Real Woman has a Cuisinart which is proudly displayed and never used. (Have you ever tried to clean one of those things? Mother does know best.)

The Real Woman longs for a cook who also does ironing and windows without so much as looking at the liquor cabinet. She know she is more apt to find the Lost Continent of Atlantis.

12 Things You Won't Find in The Real Woman's Kitchen

1. Chili Dogs
2. Iron City Beer
3. Head Cheese
4. Blood Sausage
5. Beer Nuts
6. Jelly Doughnuts
7. Pickled Pigs Feet
8. Tripe
9. Cotton Candy
10. Beef Jerky
11. Dinty Moore Beef Stew
12. Spanish Fly

"*I like to keep him guessing. One night The Girl Next Door,
the next The Whore of Babylon.*"

The Real Woman's Love Life

Real Women are Romantics. Capital R Romantics. Real Women are in love with love. They agree with Elizabeth Taylor that a girl should marry for love, and keep on getting married until she finds it (although they hope it won't take them quite as many tries).

Real Women want to be courted with flowers, candy, baubles, gypsy violin music, candlelight and champagne, soft words of wooing. They seldom succumb to the blandishments of a strange man who introduces himself on a streetcorner by saying, "Hubba, hubba, Toots! How's about a noonie?"

On the other hand, the Real Woman is enough of a Romantic to believe in Love at First Sight. If the man is a dead ringer for Robert Redford, who cares if his courting technique is a trifle abrupt.

By the same token, a Real Woman isn't afraid to let a man know that she's interested in him. She may do this by making eye contact and smiling. (But no matter *what* the man's got, she never lets her eyes stray any further down. That would be vulgar, and Real Women are never vulgar.) Or she may attract his attention with a casual observation such as "What's a nice man like you doing in a place like this?"

Real Women do not subscribe to computerized dating services. They don't need to. And even if they did, they would never dream of entrusting something so precious and deeply personal as their lovelife to anything as heartless as a computer.

Not every Real Woman is a ravishing beauty. Nor has a perfect figure. But all Real Women are sexy. They are confident of their femininity, comfortable with their bodies. Only occasionally do they wish for a little less of this, a little more of that.

Real Women prefer not to go right to bed on the first date. They don't like to be rushed; they would rather have time for their fantasies about a particular man to ripen.

Or they may hesitate to get so involved so quickly with the man, especially if he is their boss or their best friend's husband. They have their scruples, after all. And Real Women *never* compromise with their scruples. Never. No, no, a thousand times, no! However, they do, when it is expedient, scrap one set of scruples for another.

Real Women are sensitive and imaginative when it comes to lovemaking. They understand the importance of atmosphere, timing, and cute underthings and nighties. No Real Woman—even if she has been married for more than twenty years— would think of doing it in exactly the same place, at exactly the same time, day in and day out. Unless, of course, she and her partner happen to find the eleven o'clock evening news a constant sexual turn-on.

A Real Woman's sexual preferences may sometimes veer in the direction of S&M. But nothing violent, mind you—just a little good, old-fashioned, harmless domination.

A Real Woman is sympathetic toward her partner's performance anxiety, particularly if it is their first time together. And if everything else about the evening has gone well, she is usually willing to give him a second chance.

A Real Woman can be perfectly ladylike in the living room, and dynamite in bed. Despite everything she was ever told about what "good girls" aren't supposed to do or feel, she enjoys sex. Loudly. And often. Both on top and on the bottom. Or somewhere in between.

Items Not Found in The Real Woman's Purse

1. **A snub-nosed revolver.**

2. **A personal vibrator.**

3. **Liquid Plumber.**

4. **Her keys.***

*Oh, they are in there all right, but you will find Judge Crater and Jimmy Hoffa before *you* find any keys in a Real Woman's purse.

Five Things Real Women Really Worry About

1. **Caffeine.***

2. **Cellulite.**

3. **Worrying too much.**

4. **Nuclear war.**

5. **Foam versus jelly.****

*Scientific busy bodies are claiming that too much caffeine is bad for the health. Real Women do not attain consciousness without their morning cups of coffee.

**What's the difference? Is either of them any good? Does *he* notice the difference? Should I enter a convent?

Real Women's
Real Tag Lines

GRETA GARBO: "I want to be alone."

MISS PIGGY: "Ma Chere Quiche, I will tell you a few of my secrets, but I must warn you it is like Heifetz how he produces music."

TALLULAH BANKHEAD: "There is less here than meets the eye."

BETTE DAVIS: "What a dump!"

TEXAS GUINAN: "Hello, Suckers."

PRINCESS DI: "Please, God, may I only have daughters. Little boys are so rough."

MAE WEST: "Is that a wad of bills in your pocket or are you just glad to see me?"

"Don't you think he's trying too hard?"

★ REAL
★ WOMEN
★ AND
★ REAL
★ MEN

Real Women
Look at Real Men

Real Women do not envy men, do not want to be like them. Real Women do not want to slog through mud in boot camp just to prove that they can. Of course they *can!* At last report, there was no trick to it.

Real Women scorn the kind of macho dolt that male supremacists tout as the "Real Man." Real Women concede that some air-brained bimbos fall for these churlish louts, but consider this evidence that the Divinity has a sense of humor.

Dostoevsky said that no man can sink so low that some woman will not love him. This is evidence that the Divinity has mercy.

Real Women live in the real world and ask no more of Real Men than that they accept their masculinity as natural, that they remain unpretentious about it, refrain from posing and preening and bullying and generally behaving like a jerk. Real Women know this is too much to ask. ✦

Real Woman's List of Real Men

Humphrey Bogart
Sam Sheppard
Jim Palmer
William S. Paley
Robert Kennedy
Joe DiMaggio
Paul Newman
Bill Murray
Lawrence of Arabia
Alexander the Great
Willie Nelson
Harrison Ford
Dashiell Hammett
Smokey Robinson

Men Who Are Trying Too Hard

Norman Mailer
Tom Selleck
G. Gordon Liddy
Roger Staubach
Bruce Feirstein

What Mother
Wanted in a Man

1. **Good forehand.**

2. **Mean martini.**

3. **Swiss bank account.**

4. **Stamina.**

What Today's Real Woman Wants in a Man

1. **Good forehand.**

2. **Mean martini.**

3. **Stock in Apple Computer.**

4. **Technique.**

Five Things Men Joke About That Real Women Don't Find Funny

1. **Mothers-in-law.**

2. **Dolly Parton's bustline.**

3. **Toxic Shock Syndrome.**

4. **Biological time clocks.**

5. **The Boston Strangler.**

Five Things Real Women Joke About That Men Don't Find Funny

1. Male menopause.

2. Sports jargon, like "drag bunt."

3. Prostate trouble.

4. The way the Quarterback gets the football from the Center.

5. Alimony.

The Real Woman's Last Laugh

As this book was about to go to press, Vanessa Trueblood called to tell me about a dream she'd had the night before.

"I was with Charles Bronson," she said brightly.

"Oh, Vanessa," I sighed enviously, "how was it? What happened? You didn't cook him quiche, too, did you?"

"Actually not. There wasn't time. You see, we were in the desert someplace. The Sahara. Or maybe it was Death Valley. Anyway, it was a blazing hot afternoon, and we were fleeing this gang of bloodthirsty bikers. Behind us engines roared and savage, inhuman cries pierced the stillness. We were on foot, running for our lives. It was terrifying, all right, but since Charles was holding one of my hands in his viselike grip, I felt safe, protected even in the midst of overwhelming danger."

"And, of course, you got away," I couldn't help interrupting.

"Well, no, not exactly. You see, all of a sudden, Charles slipped and fell, nearly dragging me down with him. I stared anxiously at his muscular, but now inert, form. Was he all right? Would he be able to move? No: he had sprained his ankle."

"Oh, Vanessa, what did you do?"

"The only thing possible," she said matter-of-factly. "Tenderly, I bent down to him. With one cool hand I quickly caressed his burning forehead. My voice was low and soothing when I spoke: 'Goodbye, darling.' "

"You mean you left him there?!" I exclaimed incredulously, nearly dropping the receiver.

"Of course," Vanessa replied crisply.

"But how could you?" I gasped.

There was a short pause on the other end of the line. Then Vanessa said, "Let me tell you one last secret, Lisa. A Real Woman always knows when to let a Real Man take the fall."